50 Foreign Pasta Dishes

By: Kelly Johnson

Table of Contents

- Spaghetti Carbonara (Italy)
- Pad Thai (Thailand)
- Japchae (South Korea)
- Fideuà (Spain)
- Manti (Turkey)
- Macaroni Pie (Caribbean)
- Soba Noodles with Tempura (Japan)
- Spaghetti Bolognese (Italy)
- Lo Mein (China)
- Pierogi with Noodles (Poland)
- Laksa (Malaysia)
- Käsespätzle (Germany)
- Soba Salad (Japan)
- Mie Goreng (Indonesia)
- Fettuccine Alfredo (Italy)
- Tteokbokki (South Korea)
- Chiles en Nogada with Pasta (Mexico)
- Bún Thịt Nướng (Vietnam)
- Pelmeni with Noodles (Russia)
- Cacio e Pepe (Italy)
- Saimin (Hawaii)
- Goulash with Pasta (Hungary)
- Greek Pastitsio (Greece)
- Butter Chicken Pasta (India)
- Shoyu Ramen (Japan)
- Vermicelli Upma (India)
- Pesto Trofie (Italy)
- Hokkien Mee (Singapore)
- Aglio e Olio (Italy)
- Fregola Sarda (Italy)
- Biryani Noodles (Pakistan)
- Palabok (Philippines)
- Lobster Mac and Cheese (USA)
- Jollof Pasta (West Africa)
- Tsukemen (Japan)

- Truffle Tagliatelle (Italy)
- Bobotie Pasta (South Africa)
- Yakisoba (Japan)
- Maccheroni alla Chitarra (Italy)
- Pho with Egg Noodles (Vietnam)
- Sopas (Philippines)
- Chuka Soba (Japan)
- Cannelloni (Italy)
- Pasta con le Sarde (Sicily)
- Baked Ziti (Italy)
- Dan Dan Noodles (China)
- Timballo (Italy)
- Orzo Salad (Greece)
- Tagliolini al Tartufo (Italy)
- Mee Rebus (Malaysia)

Spaghetti Carbonara (Italy)

Ingredients:

- 12 oz spaghetti
- 4 oz pancetta, diced
- 2 large eggs
- ½ cup grated Pecorino Romano
- ½ cup grated Parmesan
- Freshly ground black pepper
- Salt
- 1 tbsp olive oil

Instructions:

1. Cook spaghetti in salted water until al dente. Reserve ½ cup of pasta water.
2. In a pan, cook pancetta with olive oil until crispy. Remove from heat.
3. In a bowl, whisk eggs, cheeses, and black pepper.
4. Toss spaghetti with pancetta, then slowly mix in egg mixture, adding reserved pasta water as needed to create a creamy sauce.
5. Serve immediately with more black pepper and cheese.

Pad Thai (Thailand)

Ingredients:

- 8 oz rice noodles
- 2 tbsp vegetable oil
- 8 oz shrimp or chicken
- 2 eggs, lightly beaten
- 3 tbsp fish sauce
- 1 tbsp tamarind paste
- 1 tbsp sugar
- ½ cup bean sprouts
- ¼ cup chopped peanuts
- 2 green onions, chopped
- Lime wedges

Instructions:

1. Soak rice noodles in warm water until soft. Drain.
2. Heat oil in a wok, cook protein of choice, then add eggs and scramble.
3. Stir in noodles, fish sauce, tamarind paste, and sugar. Toss to combine.
4. Add bean sprouts and cook for 1-2 minutes.
5. Serve garnished with peanuts, green onions, and lime wedges.

Japchae (South Korea)

Ingredients:

- 8 oz sweet potato noodles
- 4 oz beef, thinly sliced
- 1 carrot, julienned
- ½ onion, sliced
- 1 red bell pepper, sliced
- 1 cup spinach
- 2 eggs
- 3 tbsp soy sauce
- 1 tbsp sesame oil
- 1 tbsp sugar
- 1 clove garlic, minced
- Sesame seeds

Instructions:

1. Cook sweet potato noodles, drain, and toss with sesame oil.
2. Cook beef with garlic, then remove.
3. Stir-fry carrots, onion, and bell pepper. Add spinach at the end.
4. In a bowl, mix soy sauce, sugar, and cooked ingredients.
5. Cook and slice eggs into strips.
6. Toss all ingredients together, top with sesame seeds.

Fideuà (Spain)

Ingredients:

- 8 oz short vermicelli noodles
- 8 oz mixed seafood (shrimp, squid, mussels)
- 1 small onion, diced
- 2 cloves garlic, minced
- 1 tsp smoked paprika
- 1 large tomato, grated
- 4 cups fish broth
- 2 tbsp olive oil
- Salt and pepper
- Lemon wedges

Instructions:

1. Heat oil in a pan, toast noodles until golden, then remove.
2. Sauté onion and garlic, then add paprika and grated tomato. Cook until thick.
3. Add seafood, then pour in broth. Stir in noodles.
4. Simmer until noodles absorb liquid.
5. Serve with lemon wedges.

Manti (Turkey)

Ingredients:

- 2 cups all-purpose flour
- 1 egg
- ½ tsp salt
- ½ cup water
- ½ lb ground beef or lamb
- 1 small onion, grated
- 1 tsp black pepper
- 1 tsp cumin
- 1 cup plain yogurt
- 2 cloves garlic, minced
- 2 tbsp butter
- 1 tsp red pepper flakes

Instructions:

1. Mix flour, egg, salt, and water to form a dough. Let rest for 30 minutes.
2. Roll out and cut into small squares.
3. Mix meat, onion, pepper, and cumin. Place small amounts onto dough squares and seal.
4. Boil manti in salted water.
5. Mix yogurt with garlic. Melt butter with red pepper flakes.
6. Serve manti topped with yogurt and butter sauce.

Macaroni Pie (Caribbean)

Ingredients:

- 8 oz elbow macaroni
- 2 cups shredded cheddar cheese
- 1 cup evaporated milk
- 1 egg, beaten
- 1 tsp mustard
- 1 tsp paprika
- ½ tsp black pepper
- ½ tsp salt

Instructions:

1. Cook macaroni, drain, and mix with cheese.
2. In a bowl, combine milk, egg, mustard, paprika, pepper, and salt.
3. Mix with macaroni and pour into a greased baking dish.
4. Bake at 350°F for 30-35 minutes until golden.

Soba Noodles with Tempura (Japan)

Ingredients:

- 8 oz soba noodles
- 1 cup tempura batter mix
- ½ cup ice water
- 8 shrimp
- 1 small zucchini, sliced
- 1 small sweet potato, sliced
- 2 cups vegetable oil
- ½ cup soy sauce
- ¼ cup mirin
- 1 tbsp sugar

Instructions:

1. Cook soba noodles, drain, and chill.
2. Mix tempura batter with ice water. Dip shrimp and vegetables in batter.
3. Fry in oil until golden.
4. Mix soy sauce, mirin, and sugar for dipping sauce.
5. Serve soba noodles with tempura and dipping sauce.

Spaghetti Bolognese (Italy)

Ingredients:

- 12 oz spaghetti
- 1 lb ground beef
- 1 small onion, diced
- 2 cloves garlic, minced
- 1 can crushed tomatoes
- 1 tbsp tomato paste
- 1 tsp dried oregano
- ½ tsp black pepper
- ½ cup red wine (optional)
- 2 tbsp olive oil

Instructions:

1. Cook spaghetti, drain, and set aside.
2. Sauté onion and garlic in olive oil. Add ground beef and cook until browned.
3. Stir in tomato paste, crushed tomatoes, oregano, and wine. Simmer for 30 minutes.
4. Serve sauce over spaghetti.

Lo Mein (China)

Ingredients:

- 8 oz lo mein noodles
- 1 cup mixed vegetables (carrots, bell peppers, cabbage)
- 8 oz chicken or shrimp
- 2 tbsp soy sauce
- 1 tbsp oyster sauce
- 1 tsp sesame oil
- 2 cloves garlic, minced
- 1 tbsp vegetable oil

Instructions:

1. Cook lo mein noodles and set aside.
2. Heat oil, cook protein, then remove.
3. Stir-fry garlic and vegetables. Add soy sauce, oyster sauce, and sesame oil.
4. Toss in noodles and protein. Serve hot.

Pierogi with Noodles (Poland)

Ingredients:

- 2 cups all-purpose flour
- ½ cup sour cream
- 1 egg
- ½ tsp salt
- ½ cup mashed potatoes
- ½ cup shredded cheese
- ½ small onion, minced
- 2 tbsp butter
- 8 oz egg noodles

Instructions:

1. Mix flour, sour cream, egg, and salt into a dough. Let rest.
2. Roll out, cut circles, and fill with mashed potatoes and cheese. Seal into dumplings.
3. Boil pierogi in salted water until they float.
4. Cook egg noodles separately.
5. Sauté onions in butter and mix with both pierogi and noodles before serving.

Laksa (Malaysia)

Ingredients:

- 8 oz rice noodles
- 1 tbsp oil
- 1 tbsp laksa paste
- 4 cups chicken or shrimp broth
- 1 can coconut milk
- 8 oz shrimp or chicken
- ½ cup bean sprouts
- 2 boiled eggs, halved
- 2 tbsp fish sauce
- 1 tsp sugar
- Fresh cilantro and lime wedges

Instructions:

1. Cook rice noodles, drain, and set aside.
2. Heat oil, add laksa paste, and cook until fragrant.
3. Pour in broth and coconut milk, bring to a simmer.
4. Add protein, fish sauce, and sugar. Cook until done.
5. Serve over noodles, topped with bean sprouts, eggs, and cilantro.

Käsespätzle (Germany)

Ingredients:

- 2 cups all-purpose flour
- 3 eggs
- ½ cup milk
- ½ tsp salt
- 1 cup shredded Emmental cheese
- 1 small onion, sliced
- 2 tbsp butter
- Fresh chives

Instructions:

1. Mix flour, eggs, milk, and salt to form a thick batter.
2. Press dough through a spaetzle maker into boiling water. Cook until they float.
3. Sauté onions in butter until caramelized.
4. Layer spaetzle with cheese and top with onions.
5. Garnish with chives before serving.

Soba Salad (Japan)

Ingredients:

- 8 oz soba noodles
- ½ cucumber, julienned
- 1 carrot, julienned
- 1 green onion, sliced
- 1 tbsp sesame seeds
- 2 tbsp soy sauce
- 1 tbsp rice vinegar
- 1 tsp sesame oil
- ½ tsp sugar

Instructions:

1. Cook soba noodles, rinse in cold water, and drain.
2. Toss with cucumber, carrot, green onion, and sesame seeds.
3. Mix soy sauce, vinegar, sesame oil, and sugar. Pour over noodles.
4. Serve chilled.

Mie Goreng (Indonesia)

Ingredients:

- 8 oz egg noodles
- 2 tbsp vegetable oil
- 2 garlic cloves, minced
- 1 small onion, sliced
- 8 oz chicken or shrimp
- 2 tbsp sweet soy sauce (kecap manis)
- 1 tbsp soy sauce
- ½ cup shredded cabbage
- 1 egg, fried

Instructions:

1. Cook egg noodles, drain, and set aside.
2. Heat oil, sauté garlic and onion. Add protein and cook through.
3. Stir in noodles, cabbage, soy sauce, and sweet soy sauce.
4. Serve with a fried egg on top.

Fettuccine Alfredo (Italy)

Ingredients:

- 12 oz fettuccine
- 1 cup heavy cream
- ½ cup butter
- 1 cup grated Parmesan
- ½ tsp black pepper

Instructions:

1. Cook fettuccine, reserve ½ cup pasta water.
2. Heat butter and cream, then add Parmesan. Stir until smooth.
3. Toss pasta in sauce, using reserved water if needed.
4. Serve with black pepper.

Tteokbokki (South Korea)

Ingredients:

- 1 cup Korean rice cakes
- 2 cups anchovy broth or water
- 2 tbsp gochujang (Korean chili paste)
- 1 tbsp soy sauce
- 1 tbsp sugar
- 2 green onions, sliced
- 1 boiled egg (optional)

Instructions:

1. Boil broth, add gochujang, soy sauce, and sugar. Stir well.
2. Add rice cakes and cook until soft.
3. Stir in green onions and cook for another minute.
4. Serve with a boiled egg if desired.

Chiles en Nogada with Pasta (Mexico)

Ingredients:

- 8 oz pasta of choice
- 2 roasted poblano peppers, peeled and chopped
- ½ lb ground beef
- ½ small onion, diced
- 2 cloves garlic, minced
- ½ cup raisins
- ½ cup walnuts
- ½ cup Mexican crema
- ½ cup milk
- 1 tsp cinnamon

Instructions:

1. Cook pasta, drain, and set aside.
2. Cook beef with onion and garlic. Add raisins and cinnamon.
3. Blend walnuts, crema, and milk into a sauce.
4. Toss pasta with poblano peppers, beef mixture, and sauce.

Bún Thịt Nướng (Vietnam)

Ingredients:

- 8 oz rice vermicelli
- 8 oz grilled pork slices
- 1 cup shredded lettuce
- ½ cup bean sprouts
- ½ cup shredded carrots
- ¼ cup chopped peanuts
- 2 tbsp fish sauce
- 1 tbsp lime juice
- 1 tsp sugar
- 1 clove garlic, minced

Instructions:

1. Cook vermicelli, drain, and set aside.
2. Grill pork slices until charred.
3. Mix fish sauce, lime juice, sugar, and garlic for dressing.
4. Serve noodles with pork, lettuce, sprouts, carrots, and peanuts. Pour dressing over.

Pelmeni with Noodles (Russia)

Ingredients:

- 8 oz egg noodles
- 12 pelmeni (Russian dumplings)
- 2 tbsp butter
- ½ cup sour cream
- 1 clove garlic, minced
- Fresh dill

Instructions:

1. Cook egg noodles and pelmeni separately. Drain.
2. Heat butter, add garlic, then toss in noodles and pelmeni.
3. Serve with sour cream and fresh dill.

Cacio e Pepe (Italy)

Ingredients:

- 8 oz spaghetti
- 1 cup grated Pecorino Romano
- 1 tsp black pepper
- 1 tbsp olive oil

Instructions:

1. Cook spaghetti, reserve ½ cup pasta water.
2. Heat olive oil, add black pepper. Stir in pasta water and cheese.
3. Toss pasta until sauce is creamy.

Saimin (Hawaii)

Ingredients:

- 8 oz ramen noodles
- 4 cups chicken or dashi broth
- 2 oz char siu pork, sliced
- 1 boiled egg, halved
- ½ cup chopped green onions
- 1 sheet nori, sliced

Instructions:

1. Cook noodles, drain, and place in bowls.
2. Heat broth and pour over noodles.
3. Top with pork, egg, green onions, and nori.

Goulash with Pasta (Hungary)

Ingredients:

- 8 oz egg noodles
- 1 lb beef chuck, cubed
- 1 onion, diced
- 2 cloves garlic, minced
- 2 tbsp paprika
- 1 tsp caraway seeds
- 1 cup beef broth
- 1 cup crushed tomatoes
- 1 tbsp vegetable oil
- Salt and pepper to taste

Instructions:

1. Heat oil in a pot, sauté onions until soft. Add garlic, paprika, and caraway.
2. Add beef, sear on all sides. Pour in broth and tomatoes.
3. Simmer until beef is tender, about 1.5 hours.
4. Cook egg noodles, drain, and serve with goulash on top.

Greek Pastitsio (Greece)

Ingredients:

- 12 oz tubular pasta (e.g., penne or ziti)
- 1 lb ground beef or lamb
- 1 onion, diced
- 2 cloves garlic, minced
- 1 cup crushed tomatoes
- 1 tsp cinnamon
- 1 cup grated Parmesan
- 3 tbsp butter
- 3 tbsp flour
- 2 cups milk
- 1 egg yolk

Instructions:

1. Cook pasta, drain, and set aside.
2. Brown meat with onions and garlic. Add tomatoes and cinnamon. Simmer for 15 minutes.
3. Make béchamel by melting butter, whisking in flour, then gradually adding milk. Stir until thick.
4. Combine pasta with half the cheese, layer with meat, and top with béchamel. Bake at 375°F for 30 minutes.

Butter Chicken Pasta (India)

Ingredients:

- 8 oz pasta of choice
- 1 lb chicken breast, cubed
- 1 onion, diced
- 2 cloves garlic, minced
- 1 tsp garam masala
- 1 tsp cumin
- ½ tsp turmeric
- 1 cup tomato puree
- ½ cup heavy cream
- 2 tbsp butter
- Salt and pepper to taste

Instructions:

1. Cook pasta, drain, and set aside.
2. Sauté onions and garlic in butter. Add spices and chicken, cook through.
3. Pour in tomato puree and simmer for 10 minutes. Stir in cream.
4. Toss pasta in sauce and serve.

Shoyu Ramen (Japan)

Ingredients:

- 8 oz ramen noodles
- 4 cups chicken broth
- ¼ cup soy sauce
- 1 tbsp mirin
- 1 tsp sesame oil
- 1 clove garlic, minced
- 1 boiled egg, halved
- 4 oz sliced chicken or pork
- ½ cup green onions, chopped

Instructions:

1. Cook ramen, drain, and set aside.
2. Heat broth, add soy sauce, mirin, sesame oil, and garlic. Simmer.
3. Serve broth over noodles, topped with protein, egg, and green onions.

Vermicelli Upma (India)

Ingredients:

- 1 cup vermicelli noodles
- 1 tbsp oil
- ½ tsp mustard seeds
- ½ onion, chopped
- 1 green chili, chopped
- ½ tsp turmeric
- 1 cup mixed vegetables (carrots, peas)
- 1 ½ cups water
- Salt to taste

Instructions:

1. Dry roast vermicelli until golden. Set aside.
2. Heat oil, add mustard seeds, onions, chili, and turmeric. Sauté.
3. Add vegetables, water, and salt. Bring to a boil.
4. Stir in vermicelli and cook until water is absorbed.

Pesto Trofie (Italy)

Ingredients:

- 8 oz trofie pasta
- 2 cups fresh basil
- ¼ cup pine nuts
- 2 cloves garlic
- ½ cup grated Parmesan
- ⅓ cup olive oil
- Salt to taste

Instructions:

1. Cook trofie, drain, and reserve some pasta water.
2. Blend basil, pine nuts, garlic, Parmesan, and olive oil into a pesto.
3. Toss pasta with pesto, using pasta water to loosen sauce if needed.

Hokkien Mee (Singapore)

Ingredients:

- 8 oz yellow noodles
- 8 oz shrimp
- 2 cloves garlic, minced
- 1 cup chicken broth
- 2 tbsp soy sauce
- 1 tbsp oyster sauce
- 1 egg, beaten
- ½ cup bean sprouts
- Lime wedges

Instructions:

1. Sauté garlic and shrimp in oil. Remove shrimp and set aside.
2. Add noodles, broth, soy sauce, and oyster sauce. Stir well.
3. Push noodles aside, cook egg until scrambled, then mix in.
4. Add shrimp back, top with bean sprouts, and serve with lime.

Aglio e Olio (Italy)

Ingredients:

- 8 oz spaghetti
- 4 cloves garlic, thinly sliced
- ¼ cup olive oil
- ½ tsp red pepper flakes
- ½ cup chopped parsley
- Salt to taste

Instructions:

1. Cook spaghetti, reserve some pasta water.
2. Sauté garlic and red pepper flakes in olive oil until golden.
3. Toss in spaghetti, add parsley, and loosen with pasta water if needed.

Fregola Sarda (Italy)

Ingredients:

- 1 cup fregola pasta
- 2 cups chicken broth
- ½ cup cherry tomatoes, halved
- 2 tbsp olive oil
- 1 clove garlic, minced
- ¼ cup grated Pecorino Romano

Instructions:

1. Toast fregola in a dry pan until golden.
2. Heat oil, sauté garlic, then add tomatoes.
3. Pour in broth and fregola, simmer until tender.
4. Stir in cheese before serving.

Biryani Noodles (Pakistan)

Ingredients:

- 8 oz vermicelli noodles
- 1 lb chicken, cubed
- 1 onion, sliced
- 2 cloves garlic, minced
- 1 tsp garam masala
- ½ tsp turmeric
- 1 cup yogurt
- ½ cup chopped cilantro
- ½ cup fried onions

Instructions:

1. Cook vermicelli, drain, and set aside.
2. Sauté onions and garlic, then add chicken and spices. Cook until done.
3. Stir in yogurt and let simmer for 5 minutes.
4. Toss in noodles and garnish with cilantro and fried onions.

Palabok (Philippines)

Ingredients:

- 8 oz rice noodles
- 2 cups shrimp stock
- 1 tbsp annatto powder
- 2 cloves garlic, minced
- ½ lb ground pork
- ½ cup shrimp, cooked and peeled
- ¼ cup crushed chicharrón (pork cracklings)
- 2 hard-boiled eggs, sliced
- 2 tbsp fish sauce
- Green onions and calamansi for garnish

Instructions:

1. Cook rice noodles according to package instructions. Drain and set aside.
2. Sauté garlic and ground pork in a pan. Add annatto powder and shrimp stock. Simmer.
3. Stir in fish sauce and cooked shrimp.
4. Pour sauce over noodles, then top with eggs, chicharrón, and green onions. Serve with calamansi.

Lobster Mac and Cheese (USA)

Ingredients:

- 8 oz elbow macaroni
- 1 cup cooked lobster meat, chopped
- 2 cups cheddar cheese, shredded
- 1 cup gruyère cheese, shredded
- 2 tbsp butter
- 2 tbsp flour
- 2 cups milk
- ½ tsp paprika
- ½ cup breadcrumbs

Instructions:

1. Cook macaroni, drain, and set aside.
2. In a pan, melt butter, whisk in flour, then gradually add milk. Stir until thickened.
3. Add cheeses and paprika, stir until melted. Fold in lobster.
4. Mix with pasta, top with breadcrumbs, and bake at 375°F for 15 minutes.

Jollof Pasta (West Africa)

Ingredients:

- 8 oz penne pasta
- 2 tbsp vegetable oil
- 1 onion, chopped
- 1 red bell pepper, blended
- 1 cup tomato puree
- 1 tsp thyme
- ½ tsp cayenne pepper
- ½ tsp curry powder
- ½ lb chicken, cooked and shredded
- 1 cup chicken broth

Instructions:

1. Cook pasta, drain, and set aside.
2. Sauté onions in oil, then add blended peppers and tomato puree.
3. Add spices, chicken broth, and simmer for 10 minutes.
4. Toss in pasta and shredded chicken, mix well before serving.

Tsukemen (Japan)

Ingredients:

- 8 oz ramen noodles
- 2 cups dashi broth
- ¼ cup soy sauce
- 1 tbsp mirin
- ½ tsp sesame oil
- 1 boiled egg, halved
- 4 oz sliced pork belly
- Green onions and nori for garnish

Instructions:

1. Cook ramen noodles, rinse with cold water, and set aside.
2. Heat dashi, soy sauce, mirin, and sesame oil. Simmer.
3. Serve dipping broth separately with noodles, pork, egg, and garnishes.

Truffle Tagliatelle (Italy)

Ingredients:

- 8 oz tagliatelle pasta
- 2 tbsp butter
- 1 tbsp truffle oil
- ¼ cup grated Parmesan
- ½ cup heavy cream
- Salt and black pepper to taste
- Shaved truffle for garnish (optional)

Instructions:

1. Cook tagliatelle, drain, and reserve some pasta water.
2. In a pan, melt butter, stir in cream and Parmesan.
3. Toss pasta in sauce, drizzle with truffle oil, and garnish with shaved truffle.

Bobotie Pasta (South Africa)

Ingredients:

- 8 oz penne pasta
- 1 lb ground beef
- 1 onion, chopped
- 2 cloves garlic, minced
- 1 tsp curry powder
- ½ tsp turmeric
- ¼ cup raisins
- 2 eggs
- ½ cup milk
- Salt and pepper to taste

Instructions:

1. Cook pasta, drain, and set aside.
2. Sauté onions and garlic, add beef, and cook until browned.
3. Stir in spices and raisins, then mix with pasta.
4. Whisk eggs and milk, pour over pasta, and bake at 350°F for 20 minutes.

Yakisoba (Japan)

Ingredients:

- 8 oz yakisoba noodles
- ½ lb chicken or pork, sliced
- 1 carrot, julienned
- ½ cup cabbage, shredded
- 2 tbsp soy sauce
- 1 tbsp oyster sauce
- 1 tsp Worcestershire sauce
- ½ tsp sesame oil

Instructions:

1. Cook yakisoba noodles, drain, and set aside.
2. Stir-fry meat and vegetables in sesame oil.
3. Add noodles and sauces, toss well before serving.

Maccheroni alla Chitarra (Italy)

Ingredients:

- 8 oz maccheroni alla chitarra pasta
- 2 tbsp olive oil
- 2 cloves garlic, minced
- 1 cup crushed tomatoes
- ½ tsp red pepper flakes
- ½ cup Pecorino Romano cheese
- Fresh basil for garnish

Instructions:

1. Cook pasta, drain, and reserve some pasta water.
2. Heat olive oil, sauté garlic, and add tomatoes and red pepper flakes. Simmer.
3. Toss in pasta, mix with cheese, and garnish with basil.

Pho with Egg Noodles (Vietnam)

Ingredients:

- 8 oz egg noodles
- 4 cups beef broth
- 1 star anise
- 1 cinnamon stick
- ½ lb beef slices
- 1 cup bean sprouts
- 2 green onions, chopped
- Lime wedges and Thai basil for garnish

Instructions:

1. Cook egg noodles, drain, and set aside.
2. Simmer broth with star anise and cinnamon for 20 minutes.
3. Pour hot broth over beef slices and noodles.
4. Garnish with sprouts, green onions, and lime.

Sopas (Philippines)

Ingredients:

- 8 oz elbow macaroni
- 1 tbsp butter
- 1 onion, chopped
- 2 cloves garlic, minced
- 1 cup shredded chicken
- 3 cups chicken broth
- 1 cup evaporated milk
- 1 cup cabbage, shredded
- Salt and pepper to taste

Instructions:

1. Cook macaroni, drain, and set aside.
2. Sauté onions and garlic in butter. Add chicken and broth, simmer.
3. Stir in macaroni, milk, and cabbage. Simmer for 5 more minutes.

Chuka Soba (Japan)

Ingredients:

- 8 oz chuka soba noodles
- 2 tbsp soy sauce
- 1 tbsp mirin
- ½ tsp sesame oil
- 1 green onion, chopped
- 4 oz sliced chicken or pork

Instructions:

1. Cook noodles, drain, and set aside.
2. Stir-fry meat in sesame oil.
3. Add noodles, soy sauce, and mirin. Toss well and serve with green onions.

Cannelloni (Italy)

Ingredients:

- 8 cannelloni pasta tubes
- 1 cup ricotta cheese
- ½ cup spinach, chopped
- ½ cup Parmesan cheese, grated
- 1 egg
- 2 cups marinara sauce
- 1 cup mozzarella cheese, shredded
- Salt and pepper to taste

Instructions:

1. Preheat oven to 375°F (190°C).
2. Mix ricotta, spinach, Parmesan, egg, salt, and pepper.
3. Fill cannelloni tubes with the mixture.
4. Spread marinara sauce in a baking dish, place filled cannelloni on top, and cover with more sauce.
5. Sprinkle mozzarella, cover with foil, and bake for 30 minutes. Remove foil and bake for 10 more minutes.

Pasta con le Sarde (Sicily)

Ingredients:

- 8 oz bucatini pasta
- ¼ cup olive oil
- 1 onion, chopped
- 2 cloves garlic, minced
- 1 can (4 oz) sardines, drained
- ½ cup fennel, chopped
- ¼ cup raisins
- ¼ cup pine nuts
- ½ tsp saffron, dissolved in 2 tbsp warm water
- ½ cup breadcrumbs
- Salt and pepper to taste

Instructions:

1. Cook pasta, drain, and reserve some pasta water.
2. Sauté onion and garlic in olive oil, then add sardines, breaking them up.
3. Stir in fennel, raisins, pine nuts, and saffron water. Simmer.
4. Toss in pasta, add breadcrumbs, and mix well.

Baked Ziti (Italy)

Ingredients:

- 8 oz ziti pasta
- 2 cups marinara sauce
- 1 cup ricotta cheese
- 1 cup mozzarella cheese, shredded
- ½ cup Parmesan cheese, grated
- 1 egg
- 1 tsp Italian seasoning
- Salt and pepper to taste

Instructions:

1. Cook ziti, drain, and set aside. Preheat oven to 375°F (190°C).
2. Mix ricotta, egg, Parmesan, salt, pepper, and seasoning.
3. Layer pasta, ricotta mixture, marinara sauce, and mozzarella in a baking dish.
4. Bake for 25 minutes until cheese is bubbly.

Dan Dan Noodles (China)

Ingredients:

- 8 oz wheat noodles
- ½ lb ground pork
- 1 tbsp Sichuan peppercorns
- 2 tbsp chili oil
- 1 tbsp soy sauce
- 1 tbsp hoisin sauce
- 2 cloves garlic, minced
- ½ tsp ginger, grated
- ½ cup chicken broth
- 2 green onions, chopped

Instructions:

1. Cook noodles, drain, and set aside.
2. Toast Sichuan peppercorns, grind, and set aside.
3. Sauté garlic, ginger, and pork. Add soy sauce, hoisin, broth, and peppercorns.
4. Toss with noodles, drizzle chili oil, and garnish with green onions.

Timballo (Italy)

Ingredients:

- 8 oz rigatoni pasta
- ½ lb ground beef
- ½ cup peas
- 1 cup marinara sauce
- ½ cup mozzarella, shredded
- ½ cup Parmesan cheese
- 2 eggs, beaten
- ½ cup breadcrumbs
- Salt and pepper to taste

Instructions:

1. Cook pasta, drain, and set aside. Preheat oven to 375°F (190°C).
2. Brown beef in a pan, add peas, marinara sauce, salt, and pepper.
3. Mix pasta with beef sauce, mozzarella, Parmesan, and eggs.
4. Grease a baking dish, coat with breadcrumbs, and layer pasta mixture.
5. Bake for 30 minutes until golden.

Orzo Salad (Greece)

Ingredients:

- 1 cup orzo pasta
- ½ cup cherry tomatoes, halved
- ½ cup cucumber, diced
- ¼ cup feta cheese, crumbled
- ¼ cup olives, sliced
- 2 tbsp olive oil
- 1 tbsp lemon juice
- 1 tsp oregano
- Salt and pepper to taste

Instructions:

1. Cook orzo, drain, and let cool.
2. Toss with tomatoes, cucumber, feta, and olives.
3. Drizzle with olive oil, lemon juice, and seasonings. Mix well.

Tagliolini al Tartufo (Italy)

Ingredients:

- 8 oz tagliolini pasta
- 2 tbsp butter
- 1 tbsp truffle oil
- ¼ cup Parmesan cheese
- ½ cup heavy cream
- Salt and black pepper to taste
- Shaved truffle for garnish

Instructions:

1. Cook tagliolini, drain, and reserve some pasta water.
2. In a pan, melt butter, stir in cream and Parmesan.
3. Toss pasta in sauce, drizzle with truffle oil, and garnish with shaved truffle.

Mee Rebus (Malaysia)

Ingredients:

- 8 oz yellow noodles
- 2 tbsp vegetable oil
- 2 cloves garlic, minced
- 1 tbsp curry powder
- ½ cup sweet potatoes, mashed
- 2 cups chicken broth
- 2 tbsp soy sauce
- 2 tbsp peanut butter
- 1 boiled egg, sliced
- Green onions and fried shallots for garnish

Instructions:

1. Cook noodles, drain, and set aside.
2. Sauté garlic in oil, add curry powder, then stir in mashed sweet potatoes.
3. Add broth, soy sauce, and peanut butter. Simmer until thickened.
4. Pour sauce over noodles, top with egg, green onions, and fried shallots.

www.ingramcontent.com/pod-product-compliance
Lightning Source LLC
LaVergne TN
LVHW061954070526
838199LV00060B/4117